3.95

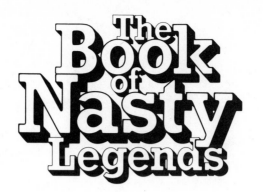

The Book of Nasty Legends

Paul Smith

Illustrated by
David Austin

Book Club Associates London

This edition published 1984 by
Book Club Associates
By arrangement with
Routledge & Kegan Paul plc
Set in Rockwell
and printed in Great Britain by
T.J. Press Ltd

To Helen, Lisa, Doc and Widdy

Contents

When someone in a pub relates a story that happened to a friend or relative of theirs we, as often as not, accept the story as true. Many of the anecdotes and stories told in such situations are, of course, true. However, have you heard about:

> The car that can be bought cheaply because it smells of the corpse that decayed in it.

> The oil company that bought, but never used, the patent on a carburettor which enables a car to get 100 miles to a gallon of petrol.

> The Rolls-Royce owner whose broken axle was repaired free of charge; the company even refused to admit that the accident had occurred.

> The motorist who delivered a hitch-hiker home only to find out later that it was the ghost of a person who had died years ago.

> The person who had a rat bone stuck in his throat as a result of eating in a foreign-food restaurant.

> The lady who put the pet cat in a microwave oven to dry; the cat exploded.

> The girl who died from the bites of insects nesting in her beehive hair-do.

You will undoubtedly be familiar with some of these stories and, perhaps, have even been told alternative versions by different people, for tales such as these have been reported throughout Europe and North America, in certain instances, for several hundred years. It will therefore come as no surprise to learn that these stories are not strictly 'true' but rather they are contemporary legends and, as such, are part of our traditional culture.

To the majority of people traditional narratives are epitomised by the classic folktales, such as *Cinderella*, or the reworked European tales presented by Hans Christian Andersen and the Brothers Grimm. Most of us, therefore, have a conception that such narratives consist of a legacy of ancient stories which are no longer relevant for our twentieth-century literate society. To a large extent this is true, for alterations in our life-styles and developments in mass media have brought changes in the way we view, practise and express our traditional culture (i.e. customs, practices, beliefs, attitudes). It is not surprising, therefore, that older forms of traditions are now no longer meaningful to us. This is, however, only one side of the story, for one of the fascinating aspects of tradition is that it constantly changes; it is very flexible and can be adapted to meet the needs of a changing world.

In addition to the many folktales that have been recorded, there also exists a parallel genre of folk narrative – legends. These are traditional prose narratives which, in the society in which they are told, are considered to be truthful accounts of what happened in the immediate past. This contrasts sharply with folktales, which are regarded as fiction and told primarily for entertainment, and myths – narratives which are considered to be truthful traditional accounts of what happened in the remote past.

Legends usually focus attention on local people and places, current events and situations. Consequently, they are far more relevant in the twentieth century than either the folktale or the myth. Of the many legends still in circulation possibly the most thriving and well-known stories are not those which deal with older ways of life or explain the existence of land forms, but rather contemporary legends. In contemporary legends the relation-ship to the past is so immediate that we are virtually concerned with the here and now. We may say, therefore, that these are traditional narratives which, in the societies in which they are told, are considered to be truthful accounts of current situations and events.

The prolific occurrence of these tales stands as a testament to their relevance in our society. Currently several hundred distinct stories are circulating and we would be hard pressed to find an individual who did not know of, or had not heard at some time, a few of these tales. Indeed, many people have a large repertoire and, in the context of the office, pub, party and locker room, actively relate them as true stories to friends and colleagues.

Many types of themes occur in contemporary legend, and stories of revenge, as in *The ten-pound car* and *The turkey neck*, contrast with the embarrassing incidents described in *The blushing bride to be*. Our dependence on technology and its consequent dangers are encapsulated in tales such as *The auto-pilot* and *Dangers of the microwave oven*. The implied warning in the latter tale is also implicit in many of the stories dealing with murder and violence. As such, it is not surprising that the legend of *The hairy-handed hitch-hiker* was frequently told as true and used as a warning during the period Sutcliffe, 'The Yorkshire Ripper', was active in the Leeds area. Similarly, the many stories of contaminated foods, unfortunate incidents, medical problems and motoring accidents all go to demonstrate that contemporary legends are alive and well and here to stay.

What then makes these stories so popular? To a large extent this is based on their relevance and on the way they function in our lives. For example, contemporary legends can provide explanations for strange behaviour and, as I have mentioned, provide warnings against involvement in particular types of situation. However, possibly one of their biggest attractions is that many are simply funny and so appeal for their entertainment value.

As to the age of these tales, few by their very nature can be said to be 'ancient'. Rather, as they are concerned with the current state of the world and the immediate past, the majority appear to have surfaced during the last thirty years. Certainly the ideas contained in some of these legends are far older. For instance, *The disappearing room* is occasionally set in the mid-nineteenth century and an obvious historical version of *The choking dog* is to be found in the Welsh legend of *Gellert* – dating from around 1458. However, in the main, long pedigrees cannot be drawn up for these legends and, to a certain extent, there is little point in attempting to discover their origin or moment of creation. The main reason for this is that it has only been in the past decade or so that we have become aware of the existence and prevalence of contemporary legends. Very little notice was taken of these stories (often regarded as flippant) and, prior to the Second World War, very few were recorded in collections of legends. Because of this, if we now wish to trace the history of any particular story we simply find a lack of evidence and can, in the main, only rely on conjecture.

Many of these legends are regarded as 'truthful accounts' of events and I would be the last person to undermine anyone's belief in them. However, accepting them as fact raises problems. Some may have a basis in truth but many others are fictions. But, having said that, why are these stories, as often as not, told as true and, more to the point, the events they describe taken to be fact? To a great extent their acceptability as 'truth' lies in their plausibility and the rational explanation of the events they describe. Both these aspects help to bolster our belief. For example, if I told you that there were giant alligators in the sewers of New York and that they had been introduced by pet-owners who flushed them down the toilet when they had grown too large, would you believe me? Many people know this story and believe it – after all, it is plausible.

Plausibility is related to truth. So just what is the relationship between belief and truth in contemporary legends? As far as the example above is concerned, in New York during the 1930s there were reports of alligators living in the sewers and a campaign was mounted to eradicate them. But, these 'monsters' were less than normal size, being only some 2 ft long. In this case, then, a relationship does exist between belief and truth and a documented event can be shown to provide a possible origin from which the legend grew. However, even if the events in New York in 1938 did not create an origin for the story, they certainly would have lent support for the plausibility of an existing legend.

However, this element of underlying truth does not always exist. For instance in *The man upstairs*, the telephone operator is allegedly able to tell that the assailant is on the extension – this is technically impossible.

However, who is to know this fact and does it matter anyway? The point to be made is that, irrespective of the extent of the underlying truth, it is the degree of plausibility that carries the day. Tales which are too fantastic are considered as fantasy and not believable. Conversely, contemporary legends, as they are concerned with everyday people, places and situations, are believable and told and retold as supposedly truthful accounts of events. This then is the nature of contemporary legend – the more ordinary the event the more believable the tale.

If we consider that one of the intentions of telling a story is to impart information then we can see that legend is only one way of putting our ideas across to others. Alternative ways of presenting these legends include rumour, gossip and jokes. The *Impeccable food* legend is an excellent example of this, for whilst this tale is frequently presented as a legend, it is not uncommon for it to occur as a rumour – 'Have you heard about the Chinese restaurant down the road? They serve up rats instead of chicken.' Similarly, I have heard someone just about to enter a Chinese restaurant comment, 'Let's try the Alsatian' – in this instance it is obviously meant as a joke. I have also seen this particular legend abbreviated in the form of graffiti. Here the phrase, 'They serve rats and mice' was scrawled on a poster for an ethnic restaurant – an implicit statement by the graffiti artist, acknowledging that the legend is very well known.

In certain cases, when these tales are related in the form of rumour and gossip, the consequences can be far-reaching. A number of ethnic restaurants, both in this country and on the continent, have had to make a public denial that their establishments constitute a health risk and that such stories have any basis in fact. In the short term, trade often declines, reputations suffer and nerves become frayed. In the long term, however, as proof can never be brought forward, in the form of the actual customers who suffered, the plausibility of the story wanes, interest declines and so the rumour ceases to be repeated. Nevertheless, since memories are short, every five to ten years the same story will surface again, told this time about a different restaurant in a different town.

While contemporary legends are related in offices, bars and at parties, they are also frequently reported as 'true stories' in the press and on radio and television. For example, the tale *Stuck on the job* has frequently appeared in the newspapers and *The husband's revenge* was reported as recently as 5 December 1982 in the *Sunday Express*. The single episode format of contemporary legends, coupled with their plausibility, gives them newsworthiness potential and, therefore, they are often reported as true. The appearance of such stories in the media is interesting in that, while on the one hand it demonstrates the gullibility of the press, on the other its reporting validates the 'truth' of the legend for the man in the street. As a result the belief/truth notion is satisfied and those oft-quoted words, 'It must be true, I read it in the paper', can be trotted out.

Besides being reported in the press the themes found in these stories are also often incorporated in films, plays and novels. In 1938 *The disappearing room* was included in the film *Verwehte Spuren* directed by Veit Harlan whilst, more recently, it provided the plot for an episode of the television series *Hart to Hart*. Similarly, *The substitute* was echoed in Hugh Mills's novel, *Prudence and the Pill*.

The increasing number of contemporary legends in circulation, added to their consistent popular appeal and regular reporting in the press, indicates that tales of this type are now a permanent part of our culture. Many of the more recent stories are concerned not just with twentieth-century life-styles but also the current fast-developing domestic technology. The story of *The spring-cleaned cat* could only exist in the twentieth century. Other legends like the *Dangers of the microwave oven* do have historical antecedents and are twentieth-century updates of older ideas. This demonstrates the strength and flexibility of tradition – it can and does adapt to a changing world. I for one am pleased by this for, like the majority of individuals, I would hate to see the great story-telling traditions of the past vanish. Besides, it is pleasant to hear a tale that makes one laugh or think and stretches one's imagination – anyway, what else would we talk about in the pub?

Paul Smith
Yorkshire 1983

As new legends, and new versions of old tales, are constantly coming to light I would be happy to hear from readers of any stories I have omitted. Please send any legends I may have missed to Paul Smith, care of:

Routledge & Kegan Paul plc
39 Store Street
London, WC1E 7DD

Acknowledgments

As the compiler of a volume which deals primarily with the traditional culture of two continents, I must first and foremost acknowledge my debt to the many people who constantly relate these tales, to friends, relatives and colleagues.

The majority of legends contained in this volume I first heard from friends and, for the wealth which they have related to me over the years, I must thank: David Austin, Ervin Beck, Marion Bowman, Georgina Boyes, David Buchan, Tony Capstick, Serafina Clarke, Derek Froome, Janie McCullock, Doc Rowe, Susan Snailum and John Widdowson.

In addition, I must gratefully acknowledge the pioneering work of a small but dedicated band of folklorists who, in spite of the conventions of their disciplines, bothered to record versions of these tales and make us aware of their importance. In particular I must acknowledge the work of Ronald Baker, Jan Brunvand, Rodney Dale, Linda Dégh, Gary Alan Fine, Bengt af Klintberg, Steve Roud, Stewart Sanderson, Alec Shearman and Graham Shorrocks.

Finally, I wish to express my sincere thanks to Lisa Warner and Helen Hartnell for their help and hindrance in preparing this volume.

The Legends

Luckless

The Persian cat and the Chihuahua

A lady, who lived down the road from a friend of mine, owned a beautiful Persian cat. She had been thinking of buying a puppy as a second pet and, on visiting the pet shop, decided upon a Chihuahua. She carried the tiny creature home very carefully, fed it and, when she went to bed later that evening, left it in the kitchen with the Persian cat.

The next morning, when she went down to the kitchen, the cat was lying there looking very contented but she could not find the puppy anywhere. She searched in every room of the house but not a trace of the dog could be found. While considering what to do next about the missing animal, she bent down to pick up the cat's bowl in order to feed it. To her horror, there in the bowl was some fur and a few small bones – all that remained of the Chihuahua. The Persian cat had eaten the puppy mistaking it for a rat.

The minced butcher

It is only in a few butchers' shops that sausages are still made by hand on the premises, and recently I heard of one butcher who still continued this practice. Every Wednesday afternoon he worked in the back room of his shop preparing sausages for the following week. He had a large grinding machine and into it he pushed the ingredients which were minced up and slowly fed into the sausage skins.

Well, this particular day, the butcher was pushing the meat in with his hand and as he worked he thought, 'This is lasting a long time.' As he reached over to add further ingredients he nearly fainted, for he suddenly realised that his hand had gone. He had minced his hand clean away and had never felt a thing.

Notes

Legends of unlucky people abound – perhaps we identify ourselves as the luckless victim. Regardless of the cause of popularity, a large proportion of the stories are concerned with forms of industrial and domestic accidents. Being brought up in a steel-producing area, as a child I frequently heard stories of people who fell into smelting crucibles or who lost limbs. Such renditions only serve to confirm the plausibility of tales like *The minced butcher*.

The performing elephant

Bill's car, a Mini, had recently been involved in an accident and he had just had it resprayed bright red. Heading for town he was surprised by the number of people about – he had forgotten that it was the day the big circus parade was due to pass through.

Parking in the main street, Bill went to do his weekend shopping. Shortly afterwards the circus parade came into view. There were the clowns, acrobats, horses, a brass band and, at the rear of the procession, a large performing elephant.

One of the tricks the elephant had been taught to do was, when the band played a particular tune, to rear up in the air and, standing on his hind legs, turn in a full circle. The trick then culminated with the elephant sitting down on a large drum painted bright red.

The elephant had just drawn level with Bill's Mini when the bandmaster, for no particular reason, instructed the musicians to strike up the tune for this trick. Up in the air went the elephant, round and round it went, then, as it always did, it sat on the nearby bright red object – unfortunately, in this instance it proved to be Bill's freshly painted car.

Notes

This delightful, and highly credible, legend has been circulating in Europe for at least the past twenty years. While told in England about a Mini, in Europe other makes of popular small car, such as Volkswagen and Fiat, suffer the same indignity. At one time the legend was so popular that a garage in Sweden, as a stunt, had publicity photographs taken of an elephant sitting on a Volkswagen.

Caught short

It was the final day on the building site and, in accordance with tradition, all the labourers went down to the pub at lunch time for a farewell drink. One of the lads was Irish and decided that he was going back to Dublin to see his family for a few months. After many farewell pints of stout he finally staggered off to the station but was caught on the way with a terrible and instant attack of diarrhoea. Only having a few minutes to clean himself up before the train left, he rushed into a gents' outfitters and purchased a pair of trousers to replace his soiled ones.

He managed to board the train, seconds before it departed, and locked himself in the toilet to clean up and change. Removing his old trousers, with no other way to dispose of them, he pushed them out of the train window. Unfortunately, when he opened the bag, he found that in his haste he had picked up the wrong parcel in the shop – this one contained a jacket belonging to another customer.

Stuck on the job

A young couple were parked in a Mini on the common one night doing a spot of courting when all of a sudden the young man, who thankfully happened to be underneath the girl at the time, let out a scream. Thinking it was a cry of passion, the girl increased her exertions only to be met with her boyfriend begging her to stop – he had slipped a disc.

Try as they would he could not sit upright so there he lay naked in the back of the Mini. In desperation the girlfriend finally phoned the ambulance service. When they arrived they also attempted to ease his pain but nothing they could do would get him upright and out of the car. In a final attempt to free the poor man, the ambulance men called the fire brigade which arrived with special cutting equipment. Before the panic-stricken girl could say or do anything, the firemen had cut the top off the car and freed her lover.

At this point the girl broke down in tears and a friendly fireman reassured her by saying, 'Well, look on the bright side, at least your boyfriend's now been released and is on his way to hospital.' 'Yes', she sobbed in reply, 'but how will I explain the state of the car to my husband?'

Notes

As one of the best-known tales of its type, *Stuck on the job* is frequently reported in the press and on the radio and television as 'true'. The humorous nature of this legend, coupled with the embarrassment suffered by the two unfortunates, all goes to make it a very appealing story. This popularity appears, however, to be limited to the British Isles – the home of the Mini. The story would, of course, not work as well if the car was any bigger. It would be interesting to speculate if the nature of the legend will change with the advent of the Mini Metro.

A blow for justice

A friend of a friend of mine went to have his hair washed and cut. He wore glasses and, as he did not want them to get in the way, he slipped them into his jacket pocket before the girl settled him in the chair and put a gown over him.

The hairdresser had finished washing his hair and had just started to dry it when my friend's friend, rather absentmindedly, slipped his glasses out of his pocket and, under the gown, started to polish them with his handkerchief.

All of a sudden, the girl drying his hair hit him across the back of the head with the hair drier and started shouting at him, 'They shouldn't let perverts like you in here.'

'What's going on?' asked the manageress, arriving at the scene of the commotion. 'I don't know,' said the poor fellow very weakly, 'all I was doing was sitting here having my hair dried and cleaning my glasses when suddenly I was assaulted.' 'Oh Christ, what have I done,' wailed the hairdresser who, turning bright red with embarrassment, continued, 'I'm ever so sorry, I thought you were masturbating under the gown – I didn't realise you were cleaning your glasses!'

Oh We Did Blush

The blushing bride to be

A young couple, who were just about to be married, stayed in one night to babysit for the girl's younger brother. After a session of petting on the sofa, the young man managed to persuade the girl to go upstairs to bed with him – for after all they were to be married soon.

They were both naked in bed when the girl suddenly remembered that she had forgotten to put the laundry in the washing machine as her mother had instructed. Rather afraid that her mother would be cross she jumped out of bed to run downstairs and quickly load the machine. Her boyfriend said he would come and help so, in the nude, they both charged down to the kitchen. As they ran through into the kitchen all the lights came on and they heard someone yell 'surprise'.

To their dismay her parents had arranged a surprise party and the kitchen was filled with a horde of relatives and friends and, last but not least, the vicar who was to marry them.

Notes

As part of a series of stories describing people surprised in the nude, this tale was first recorded in Kentucky in 1927. Since then it has been persistently reported in America and Canada. Related legends, covering such embarrassing situations as the girl who goes swimming in a new costume only to find that the fabric becomes transparent when wet, also abound. From the number and variety of this group of legends it would appear that sexually embarrassing situations are frequently experienced by many of us – why else would we believe all these tales?

Not your lucky night

It was the day of the boss's birthday and his secretary, quite out of the blue, invited him round to her flat after work for a drink. She was a very good-looking woman and the boss had always been attracted to her, though neither had ever made any advance to the other.

Thinking that she was for once giving him the come on, by the time they arrived at her flat, he had totally misinterpreted her intentions. So, when she gave him a large whisky and said that she must just slip into the bedroom to see to a few things, his expectations rose and, in a mad moment, he removed his clothing and stood ready and waiting for her return.

He was in fact standing just in his socks when his wife, children, friends and colleagues burst out of the bedroom carrying a large cake and singing 'Happy Birthday to you . . . .'

At the end of a long and very tiring business meeting an American executive boarded the sleeper train to travel south for his appointment the next day. Sitting relaxing in the bar, he started chatting to a tall and very attractive woman. After much conversation, and several drinks, she invited him back to her berth for a 'little nightcap'. Eventually, as he had expected, the 'little nightcap' turned into a session of love-making and they both retired into the woman's bunk.

When he awoke in the morning the woman was gone and all around him was still and quiet. Jumping out of the bunk he looked out of the window only to discover that the coach he was in had been cut out and left in a remote siding. He turned hurriedly to get dressed only to discover that the woman had stolen all his money and clothes and left him alone, naked and penniless.

Notes

Essentially a story based in the USA, versions have been circulating amongst railroad workers and passengers since around 1940. The system of rail routes employed in Britain, in the main, alleviates the need to pull carriages into sidings overnight. However, think how many stories you have heard of people going to sleep and missing stations or ending up in the sidings for the night.

Overexposure

As they left the caravan site just after dawn that morning the wife stayed in bed in the trailer while her husband drove. As she drowsily awoke she felt the motion of the trailer stop and, thinking they had reached their destination, a remote and secluded site in the hills, she stepped out of the caravan in her sleeping attire – her birthday suit.

At that precise moment, the trailer sped away and there she was left, stark naked, at a set of traffic lights in the middle of town during the morning rush-hour.

Notes

This very popular legend has been widely recorded since the 1960s on both sides of the Atlantic. It has even been reported as 'a true story' in the *Weekend Camper* (1973). The simplicity and humour of the tale has meant that it has been incorporated into many other mediated forms of entertainment. For example, it was used as the climactic incident in the Doris Day film *With Six You Get Egg Roll*. Similarly, it was incorporated into *The Likely Lads* film.

A cold surprise

Early one morning a friend of my brother went downstairs in his short karate-style dressing-gown to collect the post. As he bent forward he suddenly felt what he thought was a hand on his bare backside – what he did not know was that it was the cold wet nose of the family's pet dog.

So great was the shock of the young man that he catapulted forward and went straight through the glass door and into the street – well, that is what he told the police when they found him.

Winded

Possibly it was the excitement of going out with Dave, her new boyfriend, for the first time. Alternatively, it could have been something she had eaten. Whatever the reason, Caroline had been stricken for the last hour with a rather bad attack of wind. By the time her date arrived it was all she could do to get from the house and into the car without disgracing herself. As Dave closed the door on her side and walked round to his, in desperation Caroline exploded with a very large and loud fart.

Dave, getting into the driving seat, appeared not to have noticed. However, turning to her and indicating towards the back seat he said, 'Let me introduce my two friends, Linda and Brian. I thought they would like to join us tonight!'

Notes

Often related as part of the cycle of embarrassing incident stories, versions of this tale have been in circulation since before the Second World War. In earlier versions the plot more closely follows that of *Not your lucky night* in that the unfortunate soul is led into a room blindfolded, unwittingly, for a surprise party. When left alone he lets out a long and loud fart. Upon the blindfold being removed he is mortified to discover that he is in the centre of a room filled with all his friends. A form of this story was incorporated into the novel by Carson McCullers, *The Heart is a Lonely Hunter* (1943).

To celebrate buying a brand new white Rover car, my friend thought he would go out for a night with the boys.

As he drove home along the motorway in the fog after consuming several pints of beer, a police car drew in alongside and forced him to pull over. The policeman asked my friend to step out of his car and was just about to tell him to 'blow into this, please', when close by there was a loud crash, followed by another and another – a multiple pile-up had started.

Ordering my friend not to go away, the policeman ran off in the direction of the noise. After a split second's deliberation my friend was in the car and on his way home. When he arrived he locked the car in the garage and told his wife, if anyone enquired where he was, to say he had been ill in bed for the last twenty-four hours.

It was later the following morning when the police called and asked to see her husband. 'I'm sorry,' the wife informed them, 'but my husband is ill in bed with 'flu.' 'Could we possibly have a look at his car?' the police asked. 'Certainly,' she replied. However, when she opened the garage doors, she was somewhat amazed to see, not her husband's white Rover, but a Rover with red and blue stripes down the sides and a blue flashing light on the roof.

Notes

This well-reported story has been circulating in the British Isles since the early 1970s. The plausibility of the story, coupled with the individual's ever present desire to 'get one over on the police', reinforce the popular appeal of this story. If only he had got away with it . . . !

The five-pound note

At work one day a lady, on looking through her purse which she had left in the staffroom, discovered a five-pound note was missing. Feeling rather upset and also angered by the loss, when she caught sight of a five-pound note in the top of a shopping bag that belonged to one of her colleagues, she immediately suspected her workmate of having stolen it.

By way of retribution the lady removed the five-pound note from the shopping bag and decided that the following day she would report her colleague to the security manager.

It was perhaps rather fortuitous that she did not report her friend when the loss was first noticed for, when she arrived home that evening, she discovered her missing five-pound note on the kitchen table where she had dropped it that morning.

Notes

Katharine Briggs in *Folk Tales of England* (1965) printed a version of this legend from Perthshire in 1912. Although popular in the British Isles, it appears to be less well known in North America. However, it does exist in the oral tradition and was reported as true in the *Indianapolis Sunday Star* (3 March 1946).

Medical Tales

A young couple were brought into the casualty department of the local hospital one evening painfully stuck together in what can only be described as a rather ambitious love-making position – as the ambulance man said, 'We had a hell of a job getting them on the stretcher, never mind getting a blanket over them.' The cause of their immediate problem was, however, not the position they had chosen but rather the circumstances that had led up to them making love. It transpired that the couple had only recently married and were in the process of renovating and decorating an old house they had bought. Earlier that evening the husband had been in the bedroom gluing the handles on to a cabinet when his wife, feeling somewhat frisky, had come in and interrupted his labours with several rather tempting suggestions. As the conversation became more passionate they fell to making love.

Just before embarking on the position in which they were found, the wife had reached out for a tube of lubricating jelly, usually kept at the side of the bed for just such moments. Unfortunately, in her passion she grabbed and applied liberally the best part of a tube of super-glue. As the doctor said, 'Your problems are only just beginning!'

Notes

Legends directly concerned with sexual techniques are rare. Circulating in both Britain and North America for at least the last ten years, this tale has many versions. In Canada, for example, it is told of two Eskimos frozen together while making love in the open air. The same themes are, however, also found in other traditional forms, such as limericks. Stanley Kramer in *The Joke's on Them* (1980) provides two relevant examples:

> An excited young man from Bombay
> Was screwing his girl in a sleigh,
> But the air was so frigid it froze his dink rigid,
> And all he could come was frappé.

> An impetuous couple named Kelly
> Are forced to walk belly to belly,
> Because in their haste they used library paste
> Instead of petroleum jelly.

A doctor was out one day playing golf with a friend, who casually enquired what the result had been of his wife's recent consultation regarding a gynaecological problem. The doctor confided that the problem had been very minor. His friend's wife had had a condom stuck in her vagina which had been easily removed. The friend was horror-struck and shouted, 'But I don't used condoms!'

The outcome of this conversation was that the friend obtained a divorce from his wife who, in turn, sued the doctor for a breach of ethics and disclosing confidential information.

The substitute

A young girl of sixteen was regularly making love with her boyfriend and, although they were using condoms, she was always scared of becoming pregnant. She would have liked to go on the pill but, as her doctor was also a friend of the family, she was afraid to approach him – an all too familiar story.

One day when tidying the bedrooms at home the girl came across some contraceptive pills belonging to her mother. Thinking that her mother probably did not need them any longer she decided to use them herself. However, just to make sure her mother did not notice, she substituted the contraceptive pills with aspirins.

The pills certainly worked for the girl. However, she was unfortunately caught out a few months later when her mother was found to be pregnant.

Notes

As one of the best known contemporary legends on both sides of the Atlantic, this story was reported in the *Guardian* (April 1965) as true. However, a variant of this theme was presented by Hugh Mills in his novel, and subsequent film, *Prudence and the Pill* (1965). Here the husband discovers his wife has a supply of contraceptive pills. He finds this matter strange as they have had a platonic relationship for some fifteen years. Switching the pills for aspirin the consequences are surprising in that not only does his wife become pregnant, but also his sister-in-law, his niece, his mistress and the maid.

The dissection

It is common practice for undergraduates at medical school, as part of their anatomy course, to undertake dissections of human corpses. Such dissections are usually made working from the feet upwards. Each week the student would work on a different section of the body and so advance from comparatively easy sections to more complicated ones, such as the head. All undissected sections of the body were kept covered and, at the end of each session, the corpses would be placed in cold storage to await further dissection at a later date.

One day, in just such a class, a young man was going through this procedure. However, when the covering was finally drawn back to allow work to commence on the head he looked down and discovered that he had spent the last few months slowly dissecting the body of his late uncle.

Notes

Many tales are related about medical students and dissection. Mostly these deal with practical jokes, such as a student shaking hands with a professor using an amputated hand – the poor professor dies of fright. This version shocks whilst at the same time it is somewhat humorous. In the case of *The dissection*, however, the full weight of the shock is thrown upon the student.

Accident-prone

It was only a few weeks ago that a friend of mine was taken to the casualty department of the local hospital suffering from a very strange combination of injuries – a severely burnt backside and two broken legs. While he was waiting for the doctor to examine his injuries, the nurse in charge of casualty prepared his admission forms which included details of how the accident occurred. Apparently my friend had gone up to use the toilet at home and, while sitting in comparative comfort, had decided to read the newspaper and have a smoke. Lighting his cigarette he threw the smouldering match into the toilet to extinguish it. Instantly he was blown up in the air and his backside severely burnt. It transpired that his wife, only minutes before, had cleaned out the toilet bowl with turpentine having mistaken the container for that of the bleach.

'Was it at that point that you sustained the broken legs?' queried the nurse. 'Oh no,' replied my friend, 'that occurred when I told the story to the ambulance men as they were carrying me down from the bathroom. They laughed so much they dropped the stretcher and I fell from the top to the bottom of the stairs and broke both my legs.'

An Oriental lady living in England visited her doctor one day complaining of stomach pains. She explained that she had been suffering from them for several months but, over the last few weeks, the pains had become very bad so, as nothing would alleviate them, she had come to his surgery for help.

The doctor gave her a thorough examination but was rather mystified because, apart from the pain, he could find nothing physically wrong with her. Deciding that a second opinion was necessary, he sent her to a specialist who finally diagnosed, much to everyone's surprise, that there was a live snake growing inside the woman's stomach.

It was thought that she acquired the snake, when it was very small, from drinking contaminated water in her home country. It is said that, as this condition is so rare in England, she had to be sent to Spain for a special operation to have the snake removed – surgeons in Spain allegedly being more familiar with this affliction because of the prevalence of contaminated water.

Notes

Numerous stories of reptiles growing inside humans have been circulating for many centuries. Although not always having the rational explanation of 'drinking contaminated water', they all contain an implied warning. The most popular group of reptiles after snakes are frogs and in a letter from Rev. Samuel Glasse to Sir Joseph Banks (27 November 1780) he describes an incident where Thomas Walker, under an emetic, vomited a live toad $2\frac{1}{2}$ inches long which crawled on the floor.

Something Nasty

Driving home one evening a couple stopped at a local fast food chicken shop. Having made their purchase they sat in the dark in the car eating the chicken portions. As the girl was eating she bit into something which felt soft and furry. Deciding that she had had enough and not liking the taste she threw the remains of the meal out of the window.

When they arrived home she looked in the mirror and discovered blood all over her mouth. Thinking it was something to do with the meal, they went back to where the chicken had been thrown out of the car and, to their surprise, they found a mouse in the batter of the fast food meal. Apparently, they were so perturbed by this event that they sued the shop and were awarded a thousand pounds in damages.

Notes

Few contemporary legends are as widely known as this unfortunate story. As part of a series commenting on contaminated foods, it has circulated widely throughout North America and the UK since the late 1960s. More often than not, it has taken the form of a rumour and, in certain instances, has had serious emotional and economic implications for the individual establishments concerned.

The propagation of such stories against fast food establishments possibly highlights the fact that, although we are eating more and more of this type of food every year, as a nation we still have an ingrained mistrust of 'production food' and are always seeking the home cooking of yesteryear.

Impeccable food

One evening several friends went out to a local Chinese restaurant for a celebratory meal. Half way through the meal one of the party suddenly started to cough and choke. Thoroughly alarmed they rushed her to hospital and she had to undergo minor surgery to remove a small bone stuck in her throat.

The surgeon who removed the bone was somewhat perplexed as he did not recognise the type of bone found. He therefore sent it off for analysis and the report came back saying that it was a rat bone.

The public health department immediately visited the restaurant to inspect the kitchens and in the fridge they found numerous tins of cat food, half an Alsatian dog and several rats all waiting to be served up.

Notes

Told of many types of ethnic restaurants throughout Europe, this legend is particularly well known in the British Isles. Circulating since the expansion of Chinese restaurants into the provinces during the 1950s, it is now so well known that it has almost ceased to have any credence and is told as a joke.

A similar tale concerns the couple who take their dog with them into a Chinese restaurant. Owing to a communication problem, instead of the dog being taken away to be fed, it is cooked and delivered to their table on a silver salver.

Again, this whole group of stories echoes our irrational fear of the unknown and exotic impinging on our traditional way of life.

Two friends stopped at a roadside café to have a snack. As it was a warm sunny day, they ordered sandwiches and cans of cola intending to sit outside and have lunch. As they drank, one of the friends commented that his cola tasted a little strange. However, he thought no more of it until he came to pour the last glassful out of the can. Much to his surprise the body of a half-decomposed mouse dropped into his glass.

The poor man was taken to hospital and, fortunately, he was found to be unharmed. Allegedly, he sued the cola manufacturers and received several thousand pounds in damages.

Notes

Particularly widespread in North America, this is one legend which may have some basis in fact rather than supposition. Since at least 1914, there have been several actions in the United States against local cola franchises by individuals who have found foreign bodies, including mice, in cola drinks. Whilst the legends themselves are not necessarily based on these isolated instances, such legal actions do provide a climate which reinforces existing legends.

In addition to the above tale, many other stories and beliefs circulate amongst children. Predominant among these is the belief that if meat is left to soak in cola overnight it will dissolve.

The perfect mousse

A young housewife was to give her first dinner party and her husband had invited several directors from his firm. As it was to be a special dinner, one of the things she intended to prepare was a salmon mousse. With this in mind, she went to the local market, purchased the necessary fish and, after cleaning it, left it on the kitchen table while she gathered up the rest of the ingredients. Returning from the larder, to her horror, she found the cat sitting on the table chewing the fish. She chased the cat away and thought – 'Well, it is not as if they will know that the cat has nibbled the fish.' Accordingly she washed and cleaned it again and got on with her preparations.

The dinner party was a great success and, as the evening came to a close, the guests went off into the night making many complimentary comments, particularly about the salmon mousse. Closing the gates after the last car had left, the couple suddenly noticed, by the side of the house porch, their cat very stiff and very dead.

Racking her brains, the young housewife tried to think what could have happened to the poor animal, when she remembered the salmon. Thinking the fish must have been contaminated, in desperation she grabbed the phone and called all the dinner guests, including her husband's directors, to explain and advise them to contact their doctors immediately. They were not amused and, in fact, several of the guests were very upset even to think that she had given them food the cat had chewed.

Just as she had made the last call the door-bell rang and there stood their next-door neighbour looking very sheepish. He explained that earlier in the evening he had unfortunately run over their cat in his drive. He was

very sorry but he had been in a desperate hurry at the time as he was on his way to meet a train. He had rung the door-bell several times in order to tell them of the accident but, unfortunately, he could not make anyone hear above the noise of the dinner party. Instead, he had left the cat by the porch – had they found it yet?

The snake bite

Several summers ago a housewife in New York suffered a very unfortunate accident while out shopping. It transpired that she had gone into a large department store to look for a wicker clothes-basket with a lid. As she looked through the baskets she kept putting her hand inside the lid and running her fingers round the rim to check that they did not have any loose canes that would snag the clothes as they were pushed in and pulled out.

While going through this procedure, all of a sudden, she gave a cry and fell to the floor. She was immediately rushed to hospital but found to be dead on arrival. On examination it was discovered that she had died as a result of a snake bite. When the baskets were checked they found a large and deadly poisonous snake in the bottom of the one she was seen to examine last. It was concluded that the snake had arrived in America having been shipped in the basket from the Far East.

A fashion-conscious young girl bought an imported dress from a major chain store in the city. She wore it a few times and everyone commented on how nice it looked. However, every time she wore it she would find herself itching and scratching her legs.

Her mother was ironing the dress one day and saw that the hem was all lumpy. While attempting to straighten it out she ripped the hem open and, to her horror, found that it was full of fleas. It was the fleas that were biting her daughter and causing the itching.

Notes

Like the majority of legends dealing with contamination and infestation this tale, known on both sides of the Atlantic, again points an accusing finger at what we perceive as the unhygienic practices of foreigners.

It is interesting to contrast the notion of infestation 'being imported' with a story recently reported in the *Daily Mirror* (10 December 1981). Here Keith Reid, Director of the National Bedding Federation, countered *Mirror Woman's* suggestion that some new mattresses were filled with old stuffing containing live bedbugs. Is this a legend in the making?

Woodworm-infested shoes

Some years ago a massive campaign was launched advertising shoes with wooden non-breakable heels – much better than the breakable plastic heels, it was claimed. Unfortunately, the manufacturers overlooked treating the shoes against woodworm and once the worms got into the heels they just ate them all away and the heels disintegrated, broke up and snapped off.

Twentieth-Century Technology

The auto-pilot

The flight ran several times a week taking holiday-makers to various resorts in the Mediterranean. On each flight, to reassure the passengers all was well, the captain would put the jet on to auto-pilot and he and all the crew would come aft into the cabin to greet the passengers.

Unfortunately, on this particular flight the security door between the cabin and the flight deck jammed and left the captain and crew stuck in the cabin. From that moment, in spite of the efforts to open the door, the fate of the passengers and crew was sealed.

Notes

This well-known tale echoes the joke regarding the fully automatic, computer-controlled, pilotless plane which, when in flight, welcomes the passengers on board and assures them 'nothing can possibly go wrong . . . go wrong . . . go wrong . . .' A similar tale is also told in the United States of the driver of a new car who switches over to auto-drive and, sitting back to read the newspaper, is the cause of a major traffic accident.

Dangers of the microwave oven I

In the kitchens of a large hotel a microwave oven had been installed. However, rather than being set at eye level, like the majority of such ovens, this one was fitted down low – almost at waist height in fact. One day a young pastry chef, who worked at a table across the aisle from this cooker, was suddenly taken ill and in seconds collapsed and died.

On investigation it was discovered that every time he stepped back to admire his handywork he stood with his back against the microwave oven door. Unfortunately, the oven door did not seal properly and over a period of time it had slowly cooked his kidneys and it was this that had eventually killed him.

Dangers of the microwave oven II

I once heard of an elderly lady who used to breed pedigree cats and exhibit them at shows. She specialised in Persian cats and their long hair always made it a difficult task to clean and groom them for showing. In order to cut down the effort involved the old lady had evolved the practice of first washing the cat, towelling it dry and then, finally, giving it a very brief warming in her electric oven.

One Christmas her cooker developed a fault and so her son, by way of a Christmas present, bought her a brand new microwave oven. On the day of the next cat show, not understanding the basic difference in the technology between an ordinary electric cooker and a microwave oven, the old lady industriously washed her prize-winning Persian cat and popped it into the oven for a few seconds. There really was no miaow, nor any noise at all from the cat, for the poor creature exploded the instant the oven was switched on.

Notes

Told about cats, dogs and babies, this sad story has regularly appeared in North America and Europe over the past few years. Pre-microwave technology versions of the legend have the individual drying the unwitting victim in a regular oven or wood stove. In Russia the tale is related of a mother bathing her baby in a tub of warm water. Placing the tub on top of the apparently unlit stove, the mother goes out and stands gossiping with a neighbour for some time. On returning indoors she is horrified to discover the draught of the open door has rekindled the fire and cooked the baby in the tub.

The spring-cleaned cat

A common tale is the one concerning the woman who one day, while spring-cleaning, inadvertently vacuumed up the family's pet cat which was asleep on the hearth-rug.

Notes

A similar story, dealing with the accidental loss of a pet, concerns a couple who move house only to lose the budgerigar in transit. When checking how well the carpets have been laid in the new house, the husband notices a lump near one edge and levels it by beating it with a hammer – end of budgerigar.

The everlasting light bulb

It was around 1920, shortly after he had married, when the old man originally purchased the light bulb from a small store in town. It appeared to be a normal light bulb. However, when after sixty years it was still going strong, he decided to write to the manufacturers and tell them of this remarkable phenomenon.

By return a reply came from the company indicating they were very interested in the bulb and would like to send someone to see it. Eventually, one of the directors of the firm called and, instead of just showing interest, offered to buy it for £1,000.

The old man, of course, refused, as the light bulb had given him good service. However, his curiosity was certainly aroused – why so much money for his light bulb? The director could provide no plausible explanation as to why they were willing to offer so much for the bulb, so the old man decided to explore this mystery further.

With the help of a solicitor friend he did a little investigating and discovered that in the 1920s this particular light-bulb manufacturer had bought and tested the patent for an everlasting light bulb. Only a few of these bulbs were made and the company, finding the invention worked, destroyed the bulbs and suppressed the idea – after all, it would have put them out of business. Unknown to the company one of the lights had accidentally become mixed up with a batch of ordinary bulbs and this was the light bulb which had lit the old man's kitchen for the past sixty years.

Notes

Stories of suppressed enterprise, of one sort or another, have regularly emerged since the end of the Second World War. In addition to everlasting light bulbs, wonder drugs and carburettors or spark plugs that would give drivers 100 miles to the gallon have also featured in such legends.

It is interesting to observe that since the western world has become somewhat more energy-conscious, the number of low-power, long-life bulbs on the market has increased and so reversed the attitudes expressed in this narrative.

The cheap video hoax

During January 1983 in Nottinghamshire and South Yorkshire many people were tempted by an offer that they could not refuse. Someone had for sale 300 video recorders. These were all a recently discontinued, but very high quality model made by a well-known company. They were such a high quality machine that even André Previn was known to endorse them. Instead of the usual price of around £400, these video recorders were being bought by the salesperson for just under £100 and were offered for sale for around £110. However, the only way he could deliver the goods was if advance orders could be obtained for all 300 machines. No money was required, all you needed to do was put your name down.

Well, of course, everyone did put their names down but, as it transpired, no video recorders appeared. I should have known better – I got caught like the rest of them!

Notes

The video 'Sale of the Century' story first appeared in South Yorkshire and the Midlands during January 1983. Practically always the same figures were quoted – 300 video machines bought for £95 each and to be sold with a £15 profit margin. Often an explanation was given in terms of 'the videos are being reduced in price because they have been discontinued and the warehouse space is needed for the new model' or 'they are part of a cancelled export order'. Thorn-EMI, the manufacturers, emphatically denied all knowledge of such transactions. However, it certainly gave them a lot of free publicity.

On the Road

It was a fine sunny day to visit the safari park so, leaving grandmother asleep in the car in one of the open areas, the rest of the family went for a walk. Grandmother was suddenly awakened by something large and squashy pawing her face. Screaming at the top of her voice and, in an attempt to get rid of the elephant's trunk sticking through the window in search of goodies to eat, she wound the car window up as fast as she could.

This was perhaps the first mistake for, instead of shutting the elephant out, she trapped its trunk. The elephant, quite understandably, was furious and promptly started to kick the side of the car. Granny screamed louder. Her screams were eventually answered by the arrival of the rest of the family and two rangers who released the elephant, but only after it had done considerable damage to the car.

The rangers were most sympathetic to the old lady's plight and took the whole family up to the lodge where they provided them all with cups of tea and large glasses of brandy to calm their nerves.

On examination, the car was rather a mess. The bodywork had been stove in down one side and the quarterlight and one front headlight were also smashed. 'Never mind,' said father, downing his third medicinal brandy, 'I'll claim for it on the insurance – that's if they believe the tale.'

Driving home along the motorway proved rather uneventful after the excitement of the last few hours. The tedium was broken, however, when father, seeing a motorist broken down at the side of the road, pulled over to see if he could help in any way. 'No thank you,' came the reply, 'I have

already phoned the breakdown services.' Before father could get back into his car, a police patrol car pulled up in front of them all and the policeman demanded to know what was going on. On being told that the first car had broken down and that father had just stopped to offer assistance, the policeman replied, in the customary way, 'A likely story. And tell me, sir,' he said turning to father, 'how come your car is all smashed up. Are you sure there hasn't been an accident here?' 'Oh no,' replied father, who then, by way of explanation, went on to relate the story of the incident in the safari park.

There was quite a lengthy pause before the policeman reached for something inside his car, turned to father and said, 'Would you mind blowing into this, sir . . .!'

The flying cow

Driving along a narrow, winding Scottish road one dark evening, a driver was somewhat surprised when his vision was completely blocked by the body of a flying cow landing on the bonnet of the car. Being totally unable to explain the phenomenon and also unable to remove the corpse from the bonnet, he pushed the car into a field and walked into the next village to report the incident to the police.

He hesitantly explained his predicament at the police station but, much to his surprise, he was not greeted with incredulity but rather with relief on the part of the police officer.

It turned out that a lorry driver had just been in to report that he thought he had hit a cow some miles back along the road. Surprisingly, when he searched for the animal its body was nowhere to be found.

The explanation was that the speed and the weight of the truck had sent the cow's body flying a considerable distance back down the road to land on the bonnet of the man's car coming up round the bend.

Notes

A similar version of this legend was told to me around 1965 and concerned another motorist driving in the dark along another narrow Scottish road. Speeding round a bend the driver was suddenly confronted with a cow standing broadside in the road. He braked quickly and, as he did so, the car bonnet dipped and went under the cow's stomach. Coming to a halt he found the cow straddling the bonnet. Unfortunately, the car was an old Austin and he had to smash the flying *A* symbol off with a rock before the cow could be slid off. What is it about cars, cows and Scotland?

The disappearing hook

I once heard a story concerning a boy scout in a local troop who only had one hand, for he had lost his other in an accident and it had been replaced with a claw. This scout, while hitch-hiking with a friend, had stuck his arm out to hitch a lift and his claw had got yanked off by a passing car. Luckily he was not injured.

Eventually, a car stopped for them and they were taken into the next town on their route. They set off to walk from where they were dropped to the campsite on the far side of town and, as they passed through the town centre, they found the missing claw in the gutter. It had stayed caught in the car door-handle and had only fallen to the ground as the car passed along their eventual route.

The driver of an articulated lorry was forever getting into trouble with the police for speeding. Time and time again he was stopped. In most instances he was let off with a warning but, as he already had two endorsements, he felt that he should take precautions. The problem was that police cars would creep right up behind him and, by driving so close, they were in a blind spot out of his line of vision.

Feeling somewhat victimised, the lorry driver fitted his vehicle with special, very wide mirrors which improved his line of vision to the extent that he could see them sitting on his tail.

While he was speeding down the local by-pass one afternoon a police car shot out of a side road and moved in right behind him. Knowing he was speeding and fearful of the consequences of being caught, the lorry driver did everything in his power to shake off the following car. All this did, however, was to increase the number of traffic offences he was committing. Finally, in desperation, he decided to brake and see if that

would stop them following him. Unfortunately, the lorry's brakes were somewhat more efficient than those of the police car and both occupants of the car were killed when it crashed into the rear of the lorry.

Notes
Widely reported in England since the 1950s, the popularity of this tale, despite its horrific consequences, is probably due to the lorry driver getting even with the police. In the *Star* (Sheffield) for February 1 1983, the following case was reported:

> Trying to avoid the consequences of having only one rear light, a fleeing Suffolk motorist smashed a following police car's windscreen with a pitchfork, later backed into the police car, his tow bar jamming the bumper.

> When the police jumped out he made off, towing the empty car, smashing into four others and ending embedded in a fifth.

> Jailing him for a month and banning him from driving for two years Judge Bertrand Richards said 'This is a serious case, although not without its humorous aspect.'

Perhaps we have here the making of another contemporary legend.

The unlucky examination

A friend of mine recently told me a story concerning a young lad who was taking his motorcycle driving test for the first time. He had gone through all the various sections of the test and was left with just the emergency stop to do.

The examiner asked him to drive round the block several times and said that he would step out into the road at one point and the boy would have to stop sharply – the expectation was that he would have to keep the motorcycle in a straight line and upright.

Well, off round the block went the boy. However, he was delayed for a while as a delivery lorry was blocking the road. As he turned the final corner to drive down to where the driving examiner had been, he was surprised to see an ambulance and the examiner being placed on a stretcher. What had happened was the examiner had made rather an error. He had stepped out in front of the wrong motorcycle and the driver, not expecting this, had knocked him down.

No claim

Returning to the car he had left in a nearby car park, a friend of a cousin of mine was rather perturbed to find one side of the vehicle all scratched and dinted. Seeing a note on the windscreen, he breathed a sigh of relief, for he thought that the culprit had left his name and address so, at least, he could make a claim for the damage against the other driver's insurance company. However, on opening the note, his relief turned to dismay when he read:

> Dear Driver,
> I have just run into your car and made a hell of a mess of it. As a crowd has gathered, I am forced to appear as if writing you this note to apologise and to leave you my name and address. As you can see, however, this I have not done.
> A Well-Wisher

The death car

One evening some years ago a friend of mine found an advertisement in the newspaper for a secondhand car. It had only one previous owner and the price was unbelievable – less than half my friend would normally have expected to pay. He immediately drove round to see the car and, finding it was still for sale, he gave it a thorough examination – after all, at that price there must be something wrong with it! Well, after giving it a good going-over, he could not find anything wrong with it except the interior had a rather peculiar smell and it had a blood stain on the front seat. In spite of this, my friend decided the car was an excellent buy, so he paid up and it was delivered the following day.

Over the next week, however, the smell in the car persisted. No matter how much he cleaned the upholstery he could not remove the stain and, if anything, the smell seemed to be getting worse. Finally, in desperation, he returned the car to the showroom. To his astonishment they offered to refund his money without question. Thinking this was strange, he asked the manager what caused the smell. The manager explained that the previous owner had committed suicide in the car while it was parked in the garage at home. Unfortunately, the body had not been found for several weeks.

Notes
Frequently reported in both the British Isles and North America since 1950, this story has been traced back, by the American folklorist Richard Dorson, to an alleged incident in Mecosta, Michigan, USA in 1938. The widespread circulation of this legend, and the fact that many alternative towns and types of car are reported, tends to indicate that the Mecosta incident possibly did not start the story but rather acted to reinforce an older tale.

Sweet Revenge

The uncharitable innkeeper

During rehearsals for the school nativity play the little boy who was playing the part of Joseph kept persistently arriving late and, more to the point, he never seemed to know his part. Eventually, as things were not going well, three days before the dress rehearsal the teacher organising the play switched the boy playing the innkeeper, a minor role, with Joseph. The boy playing the innkeeper was, of course, delighted but the other child was very disgruntled.

The dress rehearsal came and all went very well except that the boy who initially played Joseph tended to be rather sulky in his new part as the innkeeper. All boded well for the first performance the next evening and, in due course, the parents and members of staff were assembled to watched the culmination of weeks of effort and hard work.

In the main the play started well and things were flowing very smoothly. Even the new innkeeper looked cheerful for a change. Mary and Joseph strolled up to the door of the inn and Joseph asked if there was a room for the night. Yes, said the innkeeper, he could find a room for Mary but, as far as he was concerned, Joseph could piss off!

The ten-pound car

Reading through the newspaper one evening, Ray came across an advertisement for a two-year-old Jaguar car in fine condition for £10. Shocked into action he immediately phoned the number given and queried whether the price was actually £10. 'Oh yes! that's correct', said the lady who answered. 'Would you like to come round and see it?'

Five minutes later Ray was standing in the lady's drive looking at his dream car – a practically mint condition Jaguar and only £10. 'Well', said Ray to the lady, 'what really is wrong with it?' 'Nothing at all', she replied, 'it's my way of getting my own back on my husband. You see, two months ago he ran off to Scotland with his secretary and last week he wrote to me to say he needed some money. As he didn't want to deprive me of anything, he suggested that the fairest thing would be to sell his Jaguar car and forward the money to him. So', she said, smiling sweetly, 'that's just what I'm doing.'

Notes
The story of the cheap car has been circulating widely in both North America and England since about 1948 and has even featured as the story line for the 'George and Lynn' cartoon strip by Michael Kelly in the *Sun* newspaper (17 March 1982). The car is very often a well-known prestige vehicle such as a Rover or Porsche with the price ludicrously low.

That will teach you to laugh!

A friend of mine pulled up at a set of automatic railway level-crossing gates that were in the down position. In front of him was a horse and cart and in front of that another car. As all three were waiting for the train to come a man walked past with his dog. The dog, for one reason or another, took a dislike to the horse and nipped it on the leg. The horse distinctly did not relish this kind of treatment and kicked out at the dog, missed and kicked the dog's owner instead. He in turn was furious. So, tying his dog by the lead to the automatic gates, before the cart driver could prevent him he gave the horse a hefty kick in return.

In some consternation, the horse reared and kicked the boot of the car in front. In panic, it then backed the cart into the front of my friend's car. While all this was going on the dog owner stood by and laughed at the chaos he had caused. This was perhaps unfortunate for, while he was laughing at the plight of the horse and the various drivers, the train passed, the automatic gates rose and his dog was hanged.

The turkey neck

Two friends one night had the unenviable pleasure of assisting a third, in a very drunken state, home from the pub. By the time they reached his house he was in a collapsed state so, without waking his wife, they laid him down on the sofa to sleep it off. On the way out through the kitchen one of the friends noticed a bowl of turkey giblets and, as they were rather put out by the companion's regular drunken antics, they decided to play a practical joke on him. They took the cooked turkey neck, opened the sleeper's flies and zipped them up again with the turkey neck hanging out.

In the morning the wife of the drunken sleeper came downstairs to see where her husband had collapsed to sleep off the previous night's excesses. Imagine her dismay when she was greeted with the sight of the cat, sitting on her husband's chest chewing merrily on what she imagined to be his penis. At this point the practical joke began to backfire for, in her shocked state, the wife fainted, fell down the stairs and broke a leg.

Martin worked as a lorry driver for a ready-mix concrete firm. Usually on Fridays he did not finish until late but, as it was his birthday, he decided to take the afternoon off and go home early. Not that it mattered very much because for all his wife appeared to care he might as well have worked twenty-four hours a day. She had not even sent him a birthday card.

As he drove into the road where he lived he was rather surprised to see a nice new shiny open-topped car parked outside his house. Wondering who the car belonged to, as he drove up he noticed, through the window, his wife deep in conversation with a man.

Martin immediately drove past and, not knowing quite what to do, returned to work. By the time he arrived he was seething with anger at the thought of his wife having an affair with someone else and, in the heat of the moment, he decided that revenge was the answer.

Quickly thinking out a plan of action, he jumped in the cab of a ready-mix concrete delivery lorry that had just been filled and headed for home. The sports car was still parked outside his house and he could see the man talking to his wife. Martin quickly brought the chute of the delivery lorry down and pumped 2 cubic feet of concrete straight inside the sports car. He then drove off to the top of the road and waited for the fun and games to start.

A few minutes later Martin was rather surprised when the visitor left the

house and walked away down the road without so much as looking at the car. However, he was even more surprised when his wife came out, saw the car, screamed and fainted.

Having got his wife back indoors, he explained what he had done and why, but she just sat and stared at him. Finally she managed to say, 'Oh! you fool, the car was your surprise birthday present and the salesman was just delivering it from the showrooms.'

Notes

Known throughout North America, England, Sweden and Norway, this tale has been reported regularly since the 1950s. As recently as 5 December 1982, the *Sunday Express* printed, as true, a version from reporter Bill Mann in San Francisco. In this instance the cement was dropped into the lover's house through an open bedroom window while he was out.

Another version of this tale has no birthday surprise but an actual lover unchaining his bicycle and cycling away from the house leaving the revenged husband wondering who the car belongs to.

Murder and Violence

Driving home alone one evening a young woman notices an old lady with a large shopping bag trying to hitch a lift in her direction. Feeling charitable, and in spite of her vow never to pick up hitch-hikers when alone, the girl stops and offers the hitch-hiker a ride. With much gratitude the old lady accepts and gets into the car. The young woman is about to drive away when she notices that her 'female' passenger has large hairy hands and wrists.

Guessing instantly that the old lady is in fact a man, she pretends to be having trouble with the car and asks 'him' to get out and check if the rear lights are working. As soon as the 'old lady' is round the back of the car the young woman immediately locks the doors and drives away.

In fear she goes straight to the police station where she is questioned and the car is searched. In the shopping bag the hairy-handed hitch-hiker has left behind, the police find a large and very sharp blood-stained axe – all ready for the next victim.

Notes

Versions of this comparatively well-known story have been circulating in England certainly since the early 1800s. The *Stamford Mercury* for 11 April 1834 reports a similar tale and Elizabeth Perkins in her book, *A Tree in the Valley*, relates how, around 1850, George Marsden of Hollowmeadows near Sheffield allegedly experienced a similar incident. In this case George attributed it to highway robbers.

The legend often functions as a warning and so, although it may lie dormant in people's memories, at times of social tension it can reappear. This story was frequently told as true and used as a warning against picking up hitch-hikers during the period Sutcliffe, the 'Yorkshire Ripper', was active in the Leeds area.

Fingers in the chain

A driver approaching the motorway slip road around dusk sees, ahead of him in the half light, two hitch-hikers. As it is raining he decides to stop and pick them up. However, when he gets closer and has slowed down he changes his mind for they are two very large and ill-dressed men and he does not like the look of them. As he accelerates to drive away, one of the men lashes out at the car with a large chain he has had hidden. Terrified, and not at this point caring about any damage to the car, the driver speeds away down the motorway as fast as he can go.

It is only when he stops at a service station that he has an opportunity to inspect the car for damage and, to his surprise, he discovers the assailant's chain wrapped around the rear bumper. When he comes to remove the offensive weapon, to his horror, he finds, tightly fastened in a knot in the other end of the chain, two fingers torn from the hand of the hitch-hiker.

Notes

Earlier parallels of this narrative are to be found in Chambers's *Traditions of Edinburgh* (1824) (1824) where a party of drunks smashed the door knocker of a house. The following morning parts of a finger, forcibly wrenched from a hand, were discovered sticking to the fragments of the knocker. Similarly, in 1752, a Swedish version was recorded in which a crofter rowing home one evening severed the fingers from a troll attempting to sink his boat.

Like many young couples still living at home the only place for Sue and Phil to do their courting was in the back of the car Phil borrowed from his father. On these evenings they would drive out to a secluded lovers lane and have a quiet, if somewhat energetic, time. One evening they were in the car following their regular athletic pursuits when, suddenly, the music on the radio was interrupted with a newsflash – a murderer had escaped from the local mental hospital. His distinguishing feature was the absence of a hand which had been replaced with a hook and people were warned to keep clear of him as he was very dangerous.

As they were parked near the mental hospital Sue became very upset and asked Phil to take her home. He replied by saying, 'Oh! don't worry I'll close all the windows and lock the doors – and besides, who would want to disturb us?' Well, Sue was not placated by this and, thinking she could hear noises around the car, she became more and more upset. Finally she broke down in tears and Phil, in spite of his previous plans, agreed to take her home.

As they drove home Sue started to calm down and the evening culminated with them having a farewell kiss in the car outside her parents' house. Having delayed the farewell for as long as possible Sue finally got out of the car and, turning to slam the door, screamed and collapsed in a faint. There hanging on the car door was the hook ripped from the hand of the escaped murderer.

HAS IT OCCURRED TO YOU THAT I MIGHT BE THE MAN WHO LOST HIS FINGERS IN THE LAST STORY

Notes

Found in both North America and Europe, this story was well known by the mid 1950s. Often told as true amongst adolescents, it demonstrates that we have, unfortunately, indoctrinated our children with a mistrust and fear of the mentally ill and a revulsion of physical disfiigurements.

Out of petrol

A young couple, not wanting to drive home along the motorway, took the back roads to their destination. Some miles past a small village they ran out of petrol. The boy decided to leave his girlfriend in the car and walk back to the village for fuel. To pass the time away she put on the radio and caught a newsflash which said, 'A patient has escaped from a high security mental hospital in the area.' Feeling rather nervous she locked the car doors and waited for her boyfriend to return.

Falling asleep, she was awakened by a steady thump, thump, thump on the car roof. The thumping became faster and faster until she almost fainted with fright.

Suddenly there were lights flashing on all around and someone was shouting to her to get out of the car and walk slowly towards him. She got out of the car only to find dozens of men all pointing guns in her direction. The man told her to keep walking towards him and not to look back. Human nature being what it is she did, of course, look back and to her horrow saw the escaped mental patient sitting on the top of the car bouncing her boyfriend's decapitated head up and down on the roof.

Notes
This charming tale of horror, although known in the UK, is often set in America during the 1960s. In fact, the earliest recorded version of the legend is as recent as 1964 from Kansas University campus.

The killer in the back seat

A young woman driving home alone one night stopped at a petrol station to fill up and check the tyres. When she had finished she decided she must quickly visit the toilet before continuing her journey. Without thinking she left the car unlocked in the air-line bay at the side of the garage and made her visit. On returning, she jumped into the car, drove away and, as she did so, noticed another car was leaving the forecourt directly behind her.

A short way up the main road she turned into a little-used minor road and, on glancing in her mirror, saw the other car had turned in after her. At this point she did not even start to consider she was deliberately being followed. However, after driving a mile or so she had the distinct impression that the car behind was following and, not only that, it was getting closer and closer.

Suddenly, and for no apparent reason, the headlights of the following car came on to full beam. Not knowing whether this was intentional or otherwise but fearing the worst, she accelerated and tried to get away from the glaring lights. However, as fast as she accelerated so did the car behind.

In desperation she turned off the road into an even smaller lane. The car behind followed with headlights blazing. By this time she was panic-stricken and, in an attempt to get away, pushed her foot to the floor. The car behind still followed.

She eventually reached home in a much distressed state and, running into the house, told her parents what had occurred and they telephoned the police. When the police arrived the car which had followed her was parked in the drive with its headlights still full on. The police made a grab for the young man who had been driving the car for he was now trying to get into the girl's vehicle. However, the young driver resisted arrest by telling the police, 'I'm sorry, it's not me you want but the man in the back of this car.' The police pulled open the girl's car door and sure enough inside they found a youth with a knotted scarf all ready to strangle the girl.

As the driver of the following car explained, he had heard on the radio that a killer, who used such tactics, was in the area. When he saw someone stealthily crawling into the back seat of the girl's car, as he did not have time to warn her, all he could do was follow with his headlights full on to deter the would-be murderer.

A young couple living in a large isolated house had gone out to a dinner party one evening and left the baby-sitter in charge of their two children. The children had been put to bed and the baby-sitter was watching the television when the phone rang. She answered but all she heard was a man laughing hysterically and then a voice saying, 'I'm upstairs with the children, you'd better come up.' Thinking it was 'one of those phone calls' or a practical joke she slammed down the receiver and turned the television sound up. A short time later the phone rang again and, as she picked it up, the unmistakable hysterical laughter came down the line and the voice once again said 'I'm upstairs with the children, you'd better come up.'

Getting rather frightened she called the operator and was advised they would notify the police and, should he phone again, could she keep him talking in order to give them time to trace the call and have him arrested. Minutes after she replaced the receiver the phone rang again and, when the voice said, 'I'm upstairs with the children, you'd better come up,' she tried to keep him talking. However, he must have guessed what she was trying to do and he put the phone down.

Only seconds later the phone rang again, this time it was the operator who said, 'Get out of the house straight away, the man is on the extension.' The baby-sitter put down the phone and just then heard someone coming down the stairs. She fled from the house and ran straight into the arms of the police. They burst into the house and found a man brandishing a large butcher's knife. He had entered the house through an upstairs window, murdered both the children and was just about to do the same to the poor baby-sitter.

Notes

Improbable, in that it is impossible for an operator to tell if calls are being made between two internal extensions, this legend has been reported in both the USA and Canada since the early 1960s. It is perhaps surprising that the tale only occasionally surfaces in Britain for annually something in the region of 250,000 nuisance calls are reported to British Telecom – many of them threatening. As one of several legends which portray the alleged experiences of baby-sitters, it is part of the current adolescent youth culture. When considered as a warning it functions similarly to the previous tale, *The killer in the back seat.*

The choking dog

A young couple lived in the suburbs of a large city. They were very fond of the city night life and used to go up to town as many evenings as possible. Every night they went out they would leave the lights on and let their large Labrador dog have the free run of the house – an adequate insurance against intruders.

One evening they returned from the theatre quite late and were shocked to find the dog choking on the floor of the entrance hall. They bundled the dog straight into the car and took it round to the vet. Whilst not too pleased at being disturbed so late at night, the vet told them not to worry, he would see to the dog and they were to return home.

On their return, as they opened the front door, the phone was ringing. It was the vet and, without any explanation, he told them to get out of the house immediately. They protested but he insisted, adding that he had called the police and would be round himself straight away to explain. Very shortly the vet arrived, closely followed by the police.

By way of explanation the vet announced that when he had examined the dog he had found that it was, in fact, choking on two human fingers. The police decided to search the house and in a cupboard in the hall they found a burglar – unconscious, with two fingers missing from his right hand.

Notes
Currently widely related on both sides of the Atlantic, this tale is contemporary in its expression of the types of fears felt by us today, such as fear of theft and violence. However, such notions are not new. A similar idea, for example, is expressed in the Welsh legend of *Gellert*, dating from 1485. Here the dog saves the child from a serpent. The father returning home and seeing the dog's bloody mouth, thinks it has eaten the child. He kills the dog only to discover the infant safe and well.

Like many young women Mary had a pet dog. The dog was not kept just for companionship but, as Mary lived alone in a remote house, to act as a guard dog to protect her. Whenever Mary went to bed at night she would lock all the doors and windows and the dog would sleep on the rug beside her bed. If, in the night, Mary heard any strange noises or was wondering if everything was all right she would often reach down and the dog would lick her hand in reassurance.

One night, while in bed asleep, Mary was awakened by a noise so she reached out for the dog who, in turn, licked her hand. Feeling safe in the knowledge that the dog was there to protect her she soon fell asleep again.

When she woke in the morning the dog was no longer in the room. Not surprised in any way by this Mary went to the bathroom to get ready for the day. On entering the bathroom she let out a terrified scream for there in the bath was the dog with its throat cut and written in blood on the wall above the bath were the words, Humans can lick hands too!

Notes

Whilst very common in both the United States and Canada, this story also occasionally surfaces in Europe. The following delightful Russian anecdote incorporates similar ideas. Here, the husband returning home late one evening gets into bed with his wife and, hearing a scratching under the bed, puts his hand down to the dog and asks, 'Is that you, Jack?' The wife's lover, who is hiding under the bed, replies, 'Yes, it's me' and licks the husband's hand (I. Il'f) and E. Petrov, *Dvenadtsat' Stul'ev*, Moscow, 1959).

Death and After

Working on the early shift a baker, perhaps not quite as awake as he should have been, fell into the dough machine. The machine was quickly turned off but sadly the baker had been killed and his body all chewed up and mixed in with the dough.

His wife was notified, of course, as was the coroner and eventually, after the post-mortem, the bakery was told they could clean out the dough machine and put it back into service. The machine was duly cleaned out and production restarted. Unfortunately, the job was not done thoroughly and a few weeks later the poor baker's widow, who had been granted free bread for her life from the company, was slicing up a loaf when she found her husband's signet ring inside.

The roast dinner

An American couple, living outside New York, went out for dinner one evening leaving their baby son in the care of a teenage baby-sitter and her boyfriend. When they returned from the dinner the boyfriend was gone and the girl appeared to be acting rather strangely. They asked the girl if everything was all right to which she replied that everything was fine and that she had stuffed the turkey and put it in the oven.

The wife was rather puzzled by this remark as she did not remember having a turkey in the house and they began to realise that something was certainly wrong. Fearing the worst, they ran upstairs to check on their son but he could not be found anywhere. In desperation they started to search the house. In the kitchen the husband noticed a funny smell and that the oven was switched on. When he looked inside to see what was burning he found the baby in the roasting dish all set out like a turkey and surrounded by roast potatoes and all the trimmings. It transpired that the baby-sitter and her boyfriend had been using 'Angel Dust', a powerful drug, and had roasted the baby while on a 'trip'.

Notes

Although related to older folk narratives dealing with similar incidents, the versions currently reported are probably told as a warning against using drugs. Versions of this unfortunate story have been reported in the United States since about 1970.

Back in the 1950s when the beehive hair-style was all the rage, one trendy girl had her long dark hair all piled up on top of her head in just such a fashion. The only way you could get it to stay in place was by using lots of lacquer. The whole style was rather time consuming to create and when you wanted to wash your hair it took hours to get it back in place again.

This meant that many girls took to washing their hair rather less frequently. The trendy girl in question, however, took things a little too far in that she did not wash her hair for months and months at a time.

One day, when she was at work, she started to complain of a splitting headache. However, she decided to work on. In the middle of the afternoon, she suddenly let out a shrill scream and collapsed. By the time the doctor arrived the poor girl was dead. When the doctor examined her to ascertain the cause of death, he realised that her hair was crawling with earwigs. They had been nesting in her unwashed hair and had eaten their way slowly through her skull, into her brain and so had killed her.

Notes

This legend appears to have originally surfaced in the 1950s when the beehive hair-style was particularly fashionable. A related story has bees smelling the girl's hair lacquer and stinging her to death – beehive hair-styles equating with bees.

A version recently told to me concerned a Rastafarian living in the hills of Jamaica who died as the result of a centipede living in his dreadlocks, puncturing his skull and entering the brain. This was reported as true in the *Montserrat Mirror* (1979). In Russia the beehive hair-style was known as *vshivyi dom*, meaning louse house.

A mix-up in the mail

Grandmother had gone out to spend Christmas with her cousins who lived in the Far East. She had not seen them for several years and was very excited about the trip. They had always been very kind to her and each Christmas they used to send a present of a jar of special spices to go in the Christmas cake her daughter made.

About two weeks before Christmas, a small airmail parcel arrived from the Far East. It had been posted on 1 December and contained what appeared to be the special spices for the Christmas cake. There was no note with it nor, surprisingly, any Christmas card. Not wanting to delay any longer, the daughter got on with the baking and produced a magnificent cake for the Christmas festivities.

It was the day after Boxing Day that a letter arrived from the cousins in the Far East. Also dated 1 December, it expressed how sorry they were to have to break the news of grandmother's death – the excitement had been too much for her. They also wrote that, because of all the arrangements that had had to be made for the cremation, they would not have time to send over the special spices for the cake this year. However, they had airmailed grandmother's ashes home and they should arrive shortly.

SHE'D HAVE WANTED TO BE CRUMBLED AT SEA !

Notes

This charming story of family life has circulated, both in the form of a joke and a legend, for many years. Certainly it was known in Michigan, USA, back in 1955 and, more recently, provided the plot for a one-act play by Pat Wilson, *Funeral Tea* (1972).

Several years ago a wealthy retired businessman died. In his will he left strict instructions that he was to be buried in the family mausoleum and that he wanted a telephone fitted inside the vault. He made this request because he had a strong belief that one day he would come back to life and he did not want to be shut up in the mausoleum unable to get out. Whilst everyone, including his wife, thought his instructions rather eccentric and nonsensical, they all had a soft spot for him and agreed to a telephone being installed.

It was some two years later that his widow was found dead by neighbours one afternoon. She had died of a heart attack whilst in the middle of a telephone call. When the rest of the relatives arrived they remembered the gentleman's strange request and when they looked in the sealed vault where he was buried they found the telephone receiver off the hook.

The disappearing room

Two spinster ladies, on a travelling holiday in France, arrived at their hotel rather late one night. They were placed in adjoining rooms and, as they were weary, both fell into a heavy sleep. Awaking in the late morning one of the ladies went into the next room to see her friend. She was perplexed to find it was not the room that she had seen the night before – the wallpaper and furnishings were all quite different and, more to the point, her friend was not there.

When she asked the receptionist where her companion was the reply came, 'What companion, madame? You arrived alone.' Rather confused the lady asked other members of the hotel staff the same question but always received the same reply, 'Madame, you arrived alone.'

Quite determined to get to the bottom of the matter, she finally went to the British Consulate who, in turn, called the police. The police reluctantly investigated what, to them, seemed a very strange story. However, much to their surprise the truth finally did come out. It transpired that the companion, shortly after retiring to bed, was taken violently ill and died. When the doctor arrived he diagnosed the cause of death as cholera. Shocked, the manager of the hotel had bribed the doctor to keep silent and an attempt to conceal the visit of the companion was planned. The body was removed, all the furnishings and fittings were destroyed and replaced. Similarly, the staff were told never to admit that anything had ever happened. Unfortunately they did not take into account the tenacity of the dead lady's friend.

Notes

Alexander Woollcott in *While Rome Burns* (1934) traced this tale to an account in the Detroit Free Press in 1889 before the trail went cold. In 1938 the director, Veit Harlan, set the story in the Paris Exposition of 1868 and created the film *Verwehte Spuren* ('Like Sand in the Wind'). This film was subsequently remade as *So Long at the Fair* (1950). More recently the idea has been used in an episode of *Hart to Hart* on British television.

The vanishing grandmother

During a camping holiday in Spain grandmother, who had been brought along with the rest of the family, died during the night of natural causes. Not wanting to bury her in a foreign country, where they might never be able to visit her grave again, the family decide to head for home and attempt to smuggle her through Spain and France and so back to England. With this in mind, they rolled grandmother's body in a carpet, tied it on to the roof rack of the car, along with the camping equipment, and started on their journey.

They drove all night and, just before breakfast, they heaved a sigh of relief as they crossed the border out of Spain and into France.

By this time all the family were very tired and hungry. As a stop for breakfast sounded a good idea, they parked the car in a side street next to a suitable café. Not wanting to leave the corpse for too long and also wishing to continue their journey as soon as possible, they ate a hasty breakfast and returned to the car. However, to their horror, their possessions has been stolen from the roof of the car including the carpet and grandmother's corpse. The funny thing is the body never did turn up.

Notes

Although a somewhat gruesome and unfortunate story, the legend has had widespread popularity throughout Europe and North America since the Second World War. More often than not set in Europe, the legend has frequently been incorporated into films and literature. For instance, Alfred Hitchcock used the theme in *The Diplomatic Corpse* and it is related over dinner to Georges de Sarre in Roger Peyrefitte's novel *La Fin des ambassades* (1953).